Beyond my wounds

I am a witness to the power of God

Heidy Mejia

RECOGNITION

I want to thank all those people who, in one way or another, were present and contributed to make this book a reality. I am especially grateful to my pastors for their support, their prayers, their advice and also for all the help you have given me, not only in this project, but in every aspect of my personal and spiritual life. Thanks to my daughters, who have been there in this process that was so difficult while I was writing, they have always believed in every word that God has given to my life and to my husband Tony Mejia for believing in me, for his prayers, for always been by side I dedicate this book, which bears part of my testimony, firstly, to the Father, to the Son, and to my faithful friend, the Holy Spirit. Thanks to his infinite love and mercy I am on my feet, and I have never been alone. I also dedicate it to each person who identifies with my testimony, to each person who has been marked and has survived, whom the enemy may have attacked with everything to destroy them and who are still standing, because they recognize that only the grace and mercy of God sustains them. Through this book I want to bring a message of faith and hope to each one of you. May it serve as a blessing and edification to your lives. God bless you all.**The names of the people mentioned in my testimony have been changed to avoid any recognition.**

CONTENTS

FOREWORD

When I met Heidy, I was able to glimpse that there was a great purpose on God's part and that He was preparing her for a ministry that would reach many people around the world. Her way of serving God shows that her heart has her Creator as its center. God chooses her to tell experiences that she will be like the voices of millions of women who have had to remain silent because of the wounds of the past. Heidy Mejia, the author of this precious jewel, writes from the depths of her soul. I had the opportunity to witness her tears, some of the times she said: <<I'm not going to make it>>, many of the times she stayed up late and felt discouraged, but I also witnessed how God strengthened her. , and inspired her to continue, understanding that this book "Beyond My Wounds" would be a blessing and a powerful tool for many people to understand that they are not alone despite the pain. It will be a book that will reborn courage and the desire to excel for many.

LICDA. Mabel M. Pizarro

ISBN: 979-8-8690-8939-7

REMOVING THORNS

THEN I HAVE FOR CERTAIN THAT THE AFFLICTIONS OF THE PRESENT TIME THEY ARE NOT COMPARED WITH THE GLORY TO COME WHICH SHOULD BE MANIFESTED IN US. ROMANS 8:18

I never thought that writing about my story would hurt so much. Perhaps for many, it is easy to take a pencil and paper and write about their experiences. However, that was not the case for me. I spent many years of my life trying to forget painful memories from my childhood. In October 2015, a woman came to me and spoke to me on behalf of God. She said, "I see a notebook. It's like a book. I see you writing a story." At that moment, I knew I had to open my wounds and speak about my testimony. It wasn't until August 2016, that I decided to start writing.

Every time I took the pencil and wrote, spiritual attacks came upon me. It became very difficult to talk about things that had marked my life in one way or another. For years, I struggled against the fear of what others would say. Doubt began to engulf my mind. Each page of this book not only carries the ink of a pen but also the tears I shed, as I relived painful moments while writing and was confronted with the reality that my wounds had not been fully healed.

I didn't understand the process I was going through when writing and the reason behind what I was feeling, which stopped me for a while. I only had the last chapter left when something strange began to happen to me: I started feeling an inexplicable pain, not only emotional but also physical. I spent sleepless nights, days without being able to eat, experiencing vomiting and pain in my bones, but medically there was no explanation.

One day, while praying, I asked the Lord, "Why am I feeling so much pain when remembering my past? Why does my body feel the pain?" At that moment, God gave me a vision. He showed me a thorn buried in a hand. I saw how the thorn didn't bother much when it was untouched, but if it remained inside, it would infect the hand. God said to me, "Do you see that wounded hand? The thorn represents those wounds you have carried for so long and haven't let anyone heal because of fear."

At that moment, He showed me the thorn being removed from the hand. I could clearly see how all the surrounding skin was torn and bleeding, but once it was out, relief was felt, and discomfort vanished: the healing process began. "That is what you are feeling when writing about things that have marked and hurt you for so many years. You have allowed Me to enter and heal those wounds you hid, which led to stagnation in your life."

This infection represents hatred, roots of bitterness, lack of forgiveness, guilt, depression, and fear, among other things. It not only affects us but also those around us. The healing process is not easy, but it is necessary.

We have all been marked in one way or another by painful events, which makes it take some people longer to open up and expose their wounds. Everything we go through is an opportunity for God to be glorified and show us His power to heal and restore. No matter how many mistakes and afflictions we go through because of sin, God will always wait for us with open arms to transform our lives so that we can be a blessing to others. We just have to take the first step and open up to His presence, allowing Him to come in and remove the thorns.

In Luke 8:43-44, the story is told of a woman who had been suffering from a flow of blood for twelve years and had spent all her money on doctors without being able to be cured. After trying everything, one day she decided to approach Jesus from behind and touch the edge of His cloak. Instantly, the flow of blood stopped. The most impressive thing about this story is not the fact that she was healed by Jesus, but the decision she made. Jesus is the Almighty and with Him, nothing is impossible. However, He will never be able to do anything in a person's life if they do not make the decision to approach Him. This woman could have stayed at home, as the laws at that time were very strict. Leviticus 15:19-33 explains that if a woman had a flow of blood, she was considered unclean and had to be excluded from society for a certain period of time, and no one could approach her. It was even to the point that if she sat on a chair, no one else could sit there.

She had lived twelve years with this condition, isolated from everyone, without family, without hope. Her situation kept her away from everyone, until one day she decided to make a decision that could cost her life. She dared to risk everything for the sake of her miracle: she didn't care what people would say or even if she would be stoned to death by others. She decided to fix her gaze on Jesus and not on men, and that's why she succeeded.

We all have a condition that, in one way or another, sets us apart from the people around us, especially those we love. However, we cannot stay locked in a room and die. Instead, we must rise and walk with our eyes fixed on the one who not only has the power to heal us but also to save us: Jesus Christ, our Lord and Savior!

MARKED INNOCENCE

JESUS ANSWERED AND SAID TO HIM: WHAT I DO YOU DON'T UNDERSTAND NOW; BUT YOU WILL UNDERSTAND IT LATER Juan 13:7

From a very young age, I had to witness the physical and emotional abuse that my father inflicted on my mother. Despite being a Christian family that attended a church in Trujillo Alto, Puerto Rico, the happiness and stability we appeared to have been nothing but a facade.

My dad was an active part of the church and the bus driver. My father was unfaithful to my mother with young people from the same church. I remember a time when we left a service and my father made the route to take the brothers to their homes, but he left a young woman for the end. He asked him to sit in the passenger seat and sent my mother to the last seat, with us. Along the way I saw my dad flirting with the young woman, who apparently was his "girlfriend". He drove to where we lived, left us in front of the house and went with her. When I arrived, my mother and he argued. I could hear the screams on the other side of the room. It was something normal in their relationship.

In 1989, shortly before Hurricane Hugo, sexual abuse by my father began. He continually went into the bathtub when it was time to bathe and made me watch him while he masturbated. I cried in fear while he covered my mouth so they wouldn't listen to me. Then he took me to the living room and sat on his legs asking for forgiveness. He told me that he loved me very much, that's why he did these things and at the same time I threatened to take our lives if I dared to talk about this with someone.

I didn't understand what was happening. I felt a lot of fear. At just four years old, he had stolen my innocence to the point where even playing with dolls became difficult for me. When it was time to take a bath, I would try to do it quickly before he entered the bathroom, but he still found a moment to touch me. During that time, I started going to preschool. I would cry constantly, vomit, and wouldn't eat. Social workers were trying to understand and figure out what was happening to me, as my behavior was not normal. I didn't dare speak out of fear that my father would fulfill his threats of hurting me more and even killing my mother.

On the other hand, the school social workers had several meetings with my parents to try to understand my behavior, but they concluded that my behavior was related to my health condition: since birth, I had allergies to milk and a very delicate stomach, so I was constantly hospitalized. Despite all this, God sent me an angel: she was my teacher. In her, I found the refuge that no one else could offer me in those moments of pain. She would stay by my side during lunchtime and naptime, as I was a lonely child. It was difficult for me to play with other kids, and I would hide under the table at school because I felt protected there.

In 1991 (I was about six years old), we moved to a residential area called Covadonga, in Trujillo Alto. At that time, sexual abuse was more intense. Part of this included forcing me to have oral sex. He didn't care if I vomited and trembled with fear. He only cared about his desires.

Every night he waited for everyone to fall asleep. He would come to my room, take off my sheet and carry me (sometimes he would drag me to his room). I would put a pink quilt on the floor and there I would lie next to it. He took off his clothes, covered my mouth very hard and abused me. When I tried to hit him or run away, he grabbed me tightly and showed me a knife that he placed under the pillow where my mom slept.

I, full of fear that it would hurt my mother, allowed the abuse and try to keep quiet. I remember constantly having the same dream: a tall character, dressed in black, with his face covered, chased me down a mountain. When he reached me, he threw me to the ground and hurt me, abused me and left me injured. I managed to escape from him. Then I could see another character, giant, dressed in white and gold and full of resplendent light. This person waited for me with his hands open and carried me until I calmed down. Then I would sit next to him and put his hands on my wounds, until they healed. Then he took me to a safe place and left.

It is incredible how at such a young age, and without knowledge of the spiritual world, I experienced so many things. In those experiences, I witnessed demons entering my room and mocking me. There was a demonic hand with long claws trying to grab me through the window. I didn't dare to ask for help to prevent my father from entering the room. Many times, I saw my father's face transform into something demonic while he abused me.

Note: It is very important for us as parents to educate our children about spiritual warfare and to seek help if they feel scared in any situation.

My father not only abused me, but my friends also became his victims. I witnessed him abusing one of my friends. She was about eleven years old, and he forced me to witness the scene. Afterwards, he threatened us. On one occasion, my father picked me up from school to have lunch with me. He took me to the car and covered the windows with sheets.

Some women walking on the street seemed to notice something strange and began banging on the windows of the car. He discreetly got out of the car. Shortly after, my mother arrived at the school, and we went to the office. After that incident, I spent some time in an orphanage called Rosa de Sharon in Guaynabo, Puerto Rico.

Eventually, I left the orphanage and returned to my parents. We immediately moved in with a Christian couple, as my friend's father had found out about my father's abuse. Moving into their house felt like being part of a family. They treated us very well, but the abuse, although decreased, did not stop. He waited for the opportune moment to carry out his macabre plan.

When my mother ran errands, I tried to stay with her, but he forced me to stay with him. As time went on, we moved to a relative's house in Gurabo, PR. At that moment, my mother was determined to separate from him. When she confronted him about what he had done to me, he quickly grabbed her by the arm and burned her with a hot iron. From that day on, she planned our escape. She took advantage of the fact that my father had gone out, and we left. We only took one bag each and walked to public transportation, heading to Río Piedras.

A friend of my mother's helped us by giving us shelter in her home for a while, thus keeping us away from everyone. This way, we prevented my father from harming us. My siblings suffered greatly every day due to my father's absence, as they didn't understand. On the other hand, I felt more at peace, although at times I missed him. I developed Stockholm Syndrome, which creates an identification with the aggressor, a bond in which the victim begins to have feelings of identification, sympathy, and liking for their abuser.

During this process, I felt guilty for everything that was happening. I felt responsible for my parents' separation and for my siblings not being able to be with my father.

CONFUSION IN MY OWN WORLD

HE HEALS THE BROKENHEARTED AND SELL YOUR WOUNDS. PSALMS 147:3

It had been a long time since my parents' separation. Every day, we would go to the department for help with abused women and children in San Juan, Puerto Rico.

In that place, they assisted in finding housing for victims of domestic violence, among other things. The divorce process had begun between my parents, and of course, many people claimed it was due to infidelity, giving little importance to the abuse I had suffered. My mother was referred to a center for battered women. During that process, I witnessed intense things happening in that place, things I did not understand, and they increased my fears, making me doubt that what my father had done to me was not normal.

In that help center, they found us an apartment with government assistance, and we were able to move to Residencial El Prado in Villa Prades, Puerto Rico. It was difficult for us to adapt, as there was a lot of violence, drugs, and weapons. After several months of living there, we found a church to attend.

My heart was filled with a great emptiness and many doubts, as I did not understand how my father, being a "Christian," had caused me so much harm. Painful stories repeated themselves, and I witnessed infidelity, lies, and manipulation. A strong sense of loneliness made me hide many things and face them alone.

I prayed daily with my siblings, both at home and in the church, but I would always question God for allowing so much pain in my heart. Sometimes, I doubted His existence and whether He truly loved me. Satan played with my mind, making me feel and think that I was a mistake, and that it was my fault that my siblings suffered from not having a father by their side and that my mother couldn't provide for us.

Sometime later, my mother was able to rebuild her life with the person who raised us. I felt a lot of confusion, rebellion, and guilt. This man, named José, decided to move in with my mother and form a family together. My life was not normal. It was very difficult to make friends and trust others. I was mocked at school for being shy and lacking self-confidence. I didn't like eating in the school cafeteria because I didn't want to be around people. I felt inferior. I hardly spoke, barely ate, and disliked looking at myself in the mirror. During recess, I would hide under the chair in the classroom. I was very thin, among many other things.

I cried frequently at school every time I remembered what happened to my dad. I couldn't help but feel hatred, but at the same time I felt love for my father. Yes, it is something strange and difficult to understand or explain, but victims of sexual abuse usually develop a codependency or affection for the person who caused the abuse. This is where the power of God comes in to break yokes and break curses and generational bonds. I remember the lack that my dad made me for many years, because he didn't have him around and because he didn't come to my school activities.

My relationship with God was growing, or rather, I was learning more and more about God's word and his great love for humanity. I made very good friends at church. In Bible school, I was able to start speaking freely, participate in children's worship, play and share with other children, which also helped me develop better academically. By the age of nine, my grades had taken a radical turn: I had all A's and competed at the district level with other schools. I won trophies, medals, accolades, and was part of various groups at school. My group of friends grew, and I wasn't as shy as before.

Time went by and my father started visiting us at our apartment in the residential area where we lived. He constantly insisted on coming back to us, but my mom was already married to José. I deeply felt the lack of affection, protection, and paternal love. My siblings missed my father and, in a way, so did I, which led to my mom allowing us to have contact with him again. Although my social life improved and it was easier for me to relate to others, as the years went by, I began to understand more the gravity of what had happened during my childhood.

Little by little, my father gained the trust of my mother, stepfather, and siblings. He would see us once a month, but only for a few hours. It seemed like everything was fine, so one day they reached an agreement: they allowed him to take us out on one Saturday a month. My father lived with my paternal grandmother.

We usually spend pleasant moments with the family, although on several occasions my dad took advantage of the fact that I was alone to have inappropriate approaches, such as kissing me, covering my mouth and touching my parts while masturbating. I am sure that the reason why he was not able to penetrate me again was because we were at my grandmother's house, which was constantly visited by family and friends.

Around the age of ten or eleven, my father married a very kind woman named Amy. She had two daughters and two sons, and she treated us with a lot of love and respect. My mother decided to give them more trust and the opportunity for us to spend time together again, both with my father and his wife, so every weekend we would go to their house to sleep over. Everything was going well for a few months, until one day my siblings went out to play outside the house. His wife asked me to wash my hair since we were all going out together. While I was showering, she went to the store, and I was left alone with my father. I was in the bathtub when he came in and pulled back the curtain. At that moment, I screamed and asked for help. He told me to forgive him, that he didn't know I was in the shower. The day continued.

We went out as a family and came back late at night. We all went to bed, but he came into my room. He tried to kiss me and take off his clothes. I yelled for help, but he covered my mouth and pulled a gun out of the first drawer of the bedside table, which was next to the bed where I slept. He put the gun to his head and threatened to kill himself. I cried. His wife got up to see if everything was okay, and my dad told him that I was only crying because he wanted to go to my mother's house. For fear of him, I said yes, that I was only crying because I needed my mom. It was very early in the morning, but they decided to take me back to my mother.

Months later, we learned that his wife had abandoned him. When he left him, he came back asking for forgiveness. My mom and stepfather talked to me a lot about forgiveness and honoring the parents, so I forgave him again. He visited us at our house, as at the beginning, until little by little he once again gained the trust of all of us.

Time passed and he began to live with another woman named Julie, who had five daughters. Again, I spent two weekends a month with him and his wife. I liked to play with Julie's girls, since I was the only woman in my house, and I didn't usually have many friends. In that home there was always an atmosphere of partying, alcoholic beverages and drugs. Sometimes, my dad gave us alcohol to drink.

I remember that one weekend he was taking care of my brothers, two of his partner's daughters and me, while Julie went shopping. My brothers went to play outside the apartment with their friends. He sent me and his wife's two daughters to bathe together. We get out of the bathroom and go into the room to comb our hair and get ready.

Suddenly my dad entered the room, pulled us by the arm one by one and began to touch us. He sat us at three o'clock on the bed, next to each other, and forced us to participate in sexual acts between us, while he touched us and masturbated. It was all dark and we were crying with fear. Scared, we went to sleep after the end. This was repeated on several occasions.

As a result of this, I was filled with confusion and had sexual acts with these young women. For a while I had doubts about my sexual orientation: I wasn't sure if I liked women, men or both. I didn't mention anything to my mom or anyone else again, because I was accustomed to him getting away with it and no one doing anything about it. Sometimes, I even felt that it was normal for a father to do those things and that I was the one who was wrong. As I grew up, I felt dirtier, more guilty, and my spiritual struggles became more intense. I started having confrontations with demons that visited my room. In those moments, I prayed more and asked God for help to overcome so much pain.

One day, my dad came to pick us up, as it was our turn to spend the weekend with him, but at the last moment, I decided not to go and stayed home with my mom. I never went with my dad and his wife again. I only saw them when they came to visit my siblings at our church and when they came to pick them up at home. I didn't dare to talk to anyone because, in any case, no one did anything about it. I felt very lonely and unprotected, until I reached my youth and thought that things would change if I began a consecrated life to God.

KNOWING MY FIRST LOVE

BECAUSE YOU, OH LORD JEHOVAH, ARE MY HOPE, MY SECURITY FROM MY YOUTH.

PSALMS 71:5

Living for God is the most beautiful experience I've had in my life. At the age of twelve, I surrendered my life to Jesus Christ. You might be wondering what I mean by that. Yes, at the beginning of this book, I mentioned that my parents were Christians, or rather, they attended church. Now I can clearly understand that being a Christian goes beyond attending or participating in a church. Being a Christian is being born again or regenerated. It simply means being born of God with the life of God. In 1 Peter 1:3 it says, "Blessed be the God and Father of our Lord Jesus Christ, who according to His abundant mercy has begotten us again to a living hope through the resurrection of Jesus Christ from the dead." It was evident that my parents had not been born again. I believe they saw the church not as a hospital for healing, but rather as a hiding place.

One day, I came to a deeper understanding of the wonders of God and realized that I couldn't do it without Him, that He alone had the power to heal my wounds and guide my steps. It was when I understood that for God to take control and help me, I needed to open my heart to Him and accept Him as my Lord and Savior. As I surrendered my life to Jesus Christ, wonderful things happened. I rejoiced in His presence and enjoyed being with the youth in campaigns, fasts, retreats, and evangelism. I loved speaking to others, especially at drug spots, about God's love. I enjoyed handing out tracts and praying for the needy.

As a result, many young people and adults came to the church, and it brought me great joy. Being in the presence of God was my place of refuge, where I felt security, joy, and peace. I longed to be filled with the Holy Spirit and be baptized in water, as the Bible says in Acts 2:38. I was taking baptism classes. One Friday, our youth group went to an outdoor youth campaign in Loíza, Puerto Rico. During the sermon, I longed for a supernatural experience with the Holy Spirit, but my mind was still bound by guilt from the past. I could see all the young people coming forward, but something reminded me of my past. I had that battle for a while. A friend, Jenny, told me to come forward with her, and that gave me the strength to go up. When I went forward, the presence of the Holy Spirit was incredibly beautiful. I couldn't stop crying. The preacher's wife approached me, placed her hand on my chest, over my heart, and told me from God's part to praise Him, that He would heal all my wounds, but He wanted my praise.

I began to worship Him and gave freedom to my

spirit. My body started trembling and my tongues became entangled. I had never felt anything like that before, and for a moment, I was scared. But she told me to worship louder, that it was the Holy Spirit. I did, and at that moment, unknown tongues came forth. I had never felt closer to God than in that instant. That night, I was not only baptized in water but also filled with the Holy Spirit and received the gift of speaking in tongues. The Holy Spirit broke me and freed me from invisible chains. It was the most beautiful experience I've had in my life, as I began to know the three great ones: the Father, the Son, and the Holy Spirit.

By having the Comforter in my life, the Holy Spirit, I could not only see the demons, but God had also placed authority in me and bestowed powerful weapons to fight in the spiritual warfare ("Behold, I have given you authority to tread on serpents and scorpions, and over all the power of the enemy, and nothing shall hurt you," Luke 10:19). Upon receiving that authority, the demons stopped intimidating me, and at the mention of Jesus' name, they fled from bodies and places. Martha was a young woman from my church with a deadly illness. My friends noticed that she hadn't attended church in a long time, and we began to worry about her. Her mother offered to have a worship service at their home since Martha didn't want to go to church. We prepared and went there. Martha didn't want to come out of her room, but the young women and I began to worship God with her mother until she came out and joined us in the service.

During the praise, I could see the demons possessing her. Her eyes started rolling, and her laughter was mocking. I placed one hand on her head and the other on her stomach, and I prayed for her. As soon as I placed my hand on her stomach, it started trembling, and the demons came out through her mouth. I saw them leaving through the living room window, but one of them, before leaving, turned towards me and gripped my leg tightly. I continued praying and rebuking it until it was gone. A couple of months later, Martha passed away, but she was set free that afternoon, and her home was also liberated.

I began to worship Him and gave freedom to my spirit. My body started trembling and my tongues became entangled. I had never felt anything like that before, and for a moment, I was scared. But she told me to worship louder, that it was the Holy Spirit. I did so, and at that moment, unfamiliar tongues emerged. I had never felt closer to God than in that instant. That night not only was I baptized in water, but I was also filled with the Holy Spirit and received the gift of speaking in tongues. The Holy Spirit broke me and liberated me from invisible chains. It was the most beautiful experience I have ever had in my life when I began to know the three great ones: the Father, the Son, and the Holy Spirit.

Having the Comforter in my life, the Holy Spirit, not only could I see demons, but God had also given me authority and powerful weapons to fight in the spiritual war ("Behold, I have given you authority to tread on serpents and scorpions, and over all the power of the enemy, and nothing shall hurt you," Luke 10:19). Upon receiving that authority, demons no longer intimidated me. By mentioning the name of Jesus, they would flee from bodies and places. Martha was a young woman from my church with a deadly illness. My friends noticed that she had been absent from church for a long time, and we began to worry about her. Her mother offered us the opportunity to hold a service at their house since Martha didn't want to go to the church. We prepared ourselves and went. Martha didn't want to leave her room, but the young women and I began to worship God with her mother until she came out of her room and joined us in the service.

During the praise, I could observe the demons that possessed her. Her eyes rolled back, and her laughter was mocking. I placed my hand on her head and another on her stomach and prayed for her. As I placed my hand on her stomach, it began to tremble, and the demons came out through her mouth. I saw how the demons left through the window in the living room, but one, before leaving, turned towards me and tightly grabbed my leg. I kept praying and rebuking it until it left. A couple of months later, Martha died, but she was set free that afternoon, and so was her house.

My mother had a recurring dream in which many

demons emerged from Martha's tomb and said they would come back for me in revenge, as God, with his power, had used me as an instrument for the liberation of this young woman. I was not afraid because I recognized it as a spiritual warfare and knew that God was taking care of me. For the first time, I was able to stay at a youth camp. In previous years, I had tried to stay, but couldn't make it past the first night: I had to be taken back home because I was scared, remembering things from my childhood. In this camp, the worship services lasted until twelve in the morning, but we enjoyed every part of it.

I met many young people from all over Puerto Rico and made many friendships, something that used to be very difficult for me. People started calling me Hermana Fueguito (Sieter on Fire) because I allowed the Holy Spirit complete freedom. The nights after the service were beautiful: we sat under the stars and all worshiped God together.

While evangelizing at drug spots with the group of young people from the church I attended, I had the opportunity to pray for many young people, young mothers, drug addicts, and more. I met a young man they called John. He lived in the residential area of Jardines de Selle, Villa Prades, Puerto Rico. For several months, we prayed for him and invited him to church, but he only accepted prayer and said he couldn't come to church because he worked at the drug spot in that area.

One Saturday, unexpectedly, we didn't do evangelism. We just went to the pastor's house to spend some time with the pastor's son since we were very good friends. This young man called us from his balcony and said, "Pray for me. I feel something bad is going to happen to me." We prayed for him and invited him again. This time he accepted and said he would come with us to church the next day, which was Sunday. It was Easter week. That Sunday, we would celebrate the Resurrection of Jesus, and the youth would present a drama. It was a great joy to see John come to church. God moved in a special way during the service. At the end of the preaching, a call was made for those who wanted to reconcile and accept Jesus as their Savior. John came forward deeply moved and accepted Jesus Christ as his Lord and Savior. With tears, he repented of his sins and received a great blessing from God.

At the end of the service, all the young people went to eat. It had been a glorious worship. John was happy and told us that he felt a peace he had never experienced before. He continued attending church for a good while. Approximately a month later, gunshots were heard near where he lived. The next day, the pastor's son gave us the sad news: he had been killed. Although it was a tragic news, deep down we had peace, knowing that he had given his life to God shortly before his death. To live for God and work for the Kingdom is the most beautiful thing a human being can experience because we have been created to serve and glorify His name, not for our own benefit, but because He is our Creator. Although I didn't understand it at that time, by simply serving God and helping others, I was being liberated from my pain.

WITHERED FLOWER

MANY ARE THE AFFLICTIONS OF THE RIGHTEOUS, BUT JEHOVAH WILL DELIVER HIM FROM ALL OF THEM.

PSALMS 34:19

As I neglected myself, I began to have friendships that were not Christian, and instead of bringing them light, I let them start extinguishing the light within me. I started middle school in Trujillo Alto, Puerto Rico, and shortly after I met José, a young man who was about three years older than me. I met him at church, during a youth activity that I attended. Since he went to church with his mom, I thought it was okay to have a special friendship with him. We got to know each other and over time I realized that I was not taking the right path. Nevertheless, I kept in touch with him. In this way, I left room for little things that were distancing me more and more from God and His purpose for me.

In school, I made bad decisions. In the moment, they seemed innocent things we did for fun (like skipping classes, cheating on exams, not turning in assignments), which caused my good grades to slowly decline. My behavior changed and I had a double life without realizing it. I would go to church, as I usually did, but I didn't have an intimate relationship with God, and the consequences were serious. In school, I met another young man named Alfredo. He was in his freshman year of high school. Our friendship developed within a group of friends. Every day, we would meet for lunch together. Sometimes he made pleasant comments that implied he wanted more than just a friendship with me.

Many people told me that he was bisexual. He had a girlfriend named María, but they hardly saw each other because she lived two hours away. A mutual friend we had, who we called Chachi, warned me that Alfredo was in a secret relationship with a man named Edgardo. Although there were things that made me think it was true, I had grown so fond of him that I didn't want to accept it.

Months passed and the school year was ending. He planned a farewell party, as his family was moving to another town in Puerto Rico. A fairly large group would attend this party, and I knew most of them. Alfredo had said it would be at his grandmother's house in the La Gloria neighborhood of Trujillo Alto. The party would take place on the last day of school in May, around 1998. We would skip classes that day, and the farewell party would start at eleven in the morning.

The day came and there were many problems getting to school: my mom, for example, didn't want my siblings and me to go to school, but I disobeyed and left. When I went outside, the school bus had already left, so I ended up walking to school (over time, I understood that God wanted to spare me from another tragedy in my life. That's why disobedience brings consequences that cause a lot of pain). I arrived at the school, and we gathered in a plaza. We sat there waiting for everyone to arrive. While we waited, Alfredo offered to buy me an ice cream and a pizza turnover. My friend Chachi told me not to take them, to wait for later since there would be lunch at the party. I noticed something strange when Alfredo, while buying the ice cream, entered the house of a man who lived near the plaza and took a while to come out. This man had a bad reputation, as it was rumored, he sold drugs, but I decided to overlook it.

I didn't listen to Chachi and ate what Alfredo had bought me. At that moment, my friend, very upset and worried, told me to go to her house because she felt that something bad was going to happen. I was about to go with her, but Alfredo convinced me to go to his party, arguing that Chachi and I would still be in the same school, while he would be moving away, and that it would be the last time we would spend together. Chachi was very upset when I decided to stay and went home.

A group of twelve people, both men and women, stayed behind. We walked to the public bus stop, where we took one that would drop us off in the La Gloria neighborhood. After several minutes passed, I began to sweat and feel dizzy. Everything was spinning around me. Some people asked if I was okay, but I could barely speak. I remember hearing Alfredo asking the driver to stop the bus so he could get off and telling the group to continue to the party at his house, that he would stop to buy me something since I didn't feel well.

Alfredo and I got off the bus, along with another boy. As we started walking, my legs weakened, and I felt even more dizzy. Though I remember very little, I can recall Alfredo guiding me towards a hill where there were abandoned houses. He told me not to be afraid, that we were just taking a shortcut through that place to get there faster.

Seconds later, I fell to the ground, weak and without

strength. My heart was racing, and I was drenched in sweat. Gradually, I began to lose consciousness. I could hear voices in the distance, and I felt Alfredo and the other person dragging me towards one of the abandoned houses. There, I completely blacked out. Sometime later, I heard the voices of many men. They were laughing, but I couldn't understand what they were saying as I was unconscious. I felt them hitting me and a sharp vaginal pain. I tried to move, but Alfredo placed something over my face, like a small towel, and pressured my nose. It had a strong smell, as if something had been added to make me fall asleep again.

The hours passed and the effect of what they had given me little by little was leaving my system. Although I was very weak, I could open my eyes and listen more clearly. I heard Alfredo talking to a man who was just standing, looking at everything and mocking him. I told him: "You see that you are homosexual, that you can't be with a woman." Alfredo defended himself by saying that it was because there were a lot of people, and he didn't like me sleeping. I saw some people pull up their pants, while they cleaned the area and discussed what they would do with me, if they left me there or took me back to school. Edgardo walked towards me while telling Alfredo: "I'm going to show you how to do this." I remember that tears came out of my eyes, but I was afraid to scream and ask for help, since there were many. I was afraid that they would beat or kill me. He proceeded to rape me. It was a lot of pain I felt. I was full of fear, and I vomited a lot. My body was shaking until I decided to call Alfredo. He came over and wiped my face a little. I asked him why he had done that to me, and he told me that it had been a bet. He also confessed to me that he liked men, and they all left.

The pain was so intense that it left me completely weakened, and I fell asleep. When I woke up, I managed to get up from the floor. I felt dizzy and confused as I looked for my clothes and got dressed. Not knowing where I was, I began to walk, shaking the earth and grass that I was carrying on my body, since I had been on the ground of that abandoned place for a long time. I felt dirty and I didn't know how to get home. I sat on a stone and cried, while I was praying. The pain, anger and shame were so overwhelming that I asked God why he allowed that to happen if he loved me. At that moment, a voice told me: "You see that you are just a sex object. No one is going to believe anything that happened. And if you tell it, even your family will be disgusted by you." That same voice told me to take my life.

I kept walking very slowly, since the pain was intense, until I found a small well of water where I could drink a little and clean the blood I had in my body. Then, I continued walking, letting myself be guided by the sound of the cars. Finally, I got on the road. It was already night. A car stopped. I had seen the driver before, but I didn't know him well. He offered me help and took me to my house, but full of fear and distrust, since I thought it could be someone from the group who had hurt me, I did not accept his help. He left, but soon after he returned. He told me: "Something doesn't allow me to leave you like this. Please, let me help you." At that moment, I accepted his help, and he took me home.

On the way I wondered what had happened to me and if I wanted something to eat. I didn't dare to tell him or accept the food, despite being very hungry. I could see in the dash of his car that it was five o'clock and something in the afternoon, almost six o'clock. It had already been several hours, almost a full day, since I had left my house for the party. I was afraid to get home, and I didn't know what I would say to my mom and my stepfather.

When I arrived, my mom was very sad and worried. When he greeted her, he told me that he had been in the emergency room, and that he had lost his pregnancy, that he was three months old. Seeing her so sad and sick, I decided not to tell her anything. I took pain medication and went to take a bath. Then I lay down in my room to try to sleep and forget a little what had happened.

Around ten o'clock at night, my older brother approached my room and informed me that Alfredo was outside the house in a car, asking for me. He wanted me to come out and talk to him. I approached the car and Alfredo was sitting in the passenger seat. In the driver's seat was a man dressed as a woman, whom he introduced as Francesca, his homosexual partner. They threatened to harm my older brother if I spoke up. Alfredo gave me instructions to write a letter to my mother, saying that I would go live with him, as I supposedly was pregnant. This ensured that my parents did not file charges against him for sexual abuse. I refused to do it and told him that I would tell the whole truth, not to look for me again. He got very upset.

Then, Francesca opened the glove compartment of the car, took out a gun, and said to me: "If you love your family, obey everything we tell you to do." Alfredo grabbed me by the waist, approached me, and bit me on one of my breasts. His bite was so strong that, when I tried to escape, it caused half of my nipple to tear, leaving me bleeding and in intense pain. They drove off quickly, almost dragging me along with them.

I was terrified, so I decided not to tell what they had done to me. Rather, I did what they told me: I wrote the letter by lying to my mom about the facts and making her believe that I had been sexually with Alfredo of her own free will. I left the letter in a place where my mom could find it. When he read it, he was very upset, he talked to my stepfather and they decided to send me to live with my grandmother in the United States, in Lawrence, Massachusetts. One day Alfredo phoned the house and my stepfather answered. Realizing that it was Alfredo, he threatened to put him in prison, so Alfredo didn't look for me again or call me anymore. A relative treated me with a lot of contempt and humiliation, which made my pain and rebellion grow even more.

Finally, the day came to move in with my grandmother. I went to church for the last time on Friday, as I would be moving the next day. Throughout the service, I couldn't stop crying. Everyone in the church assumed I was sad about leaving my loved ones behind. Only God knew the true cause of my pain. At the end of the service, I approached the front to have them pray for me and poured out my heart at the altar. I bid farewell to all the young people without knowing when I would see them again.

LOST IN THE PAIN

AND HE SAID TO ME: MY GRACE IS ENOUGH FOR YOU, BECAUSE MY POWER IS PERFECTED IN WEAKNESS. THEREFORE, GLADLY I WILL GLORY MORE THAN IN MY WEAKNESSES, SO THAT THE POWER OF CHRIST." 2 CORINTHIANS 12:9

My dream had always been to live with my maternal grandmother, as I always found protection in her. Every time she traveled to Puerto Rico to visit us on vacation, my father wouldn't abuse me during that time.

I had mixed feelings about my grandmother and aunts when moving from Puerto Rico to Massachusetts. On one hand, I felt happy because I enjoyed being with them, but on the other hand, I also felt a lot of sadness for what I had experienced and for having to be away from my mother and siblings.

The first few weeks were filled with laughter, as I spent a pleasant time with my relatives. We went out for walks frequently and did many fun activities. But at night, when I was alone in my room, it was inevitable to remember everything that had happened since my childhood. I felt that my life was a mistake, that I should never have been born, and that God did not love me.

Every night I had nightmares, accompanied by very painful memories. I fought in my dreams to protect myself from the harm that had been done to me. I would wake up scared, trembling with fear, screaming, sweating, and asking for help. My grandmother would always come to my room to see what was happening and would hug me until I calmed down. One day, I told my grandmother what had really happened with Alfredo. She comforted me and told me that I had to talk about it with my mom and other close family members, that I needed to tell them the whole truth of what had happened with Alfredo. When I discussed it, some didn't believe me and thought I was making up that story to make myself look good. However, the majority sought ways to help me forget and heal.

Pain, frustration, depression and the feeling of guilt were more and more intense. That's how the days went by, and I kept sinking into deep pain. I felt like not going to church anymore and taking my life. Months passed and I started school, in 8th grade. Little by little I became extremely rebellious. Then the pain had become an insatiable desire for revenge. I lost interest in doing positive things: I just wanted to go to parties, etc. As time went by, I started drinking alcohol.

Sometimes I would cut classes and run away to go with my friends. It was in this way that I met many people who, for the most part, were men. I smoked cigarettes and I tried to experience new and more and more risky things. I felt a desire for revenge and a lot of hatred, so I flirted with all the men who approached me and played with their feelings. I had no respect for them. During the course of that school year, many things happened to me. In addition to drinking alcohol, I took drug: first with marijuana and then with cocaine, etc. Every day I was more tied up. I was trying to hide my reality, but in truth I was just sinking more and more.

Very often I heard the demons calling me by my name and telling me to kill me, that that was the only way to end everything. I saw the demons enter my room and make fun of me. Sometimes I even felt like they were touching me. Because of my lack of knowledge, I thought I was going crazy. There were so many attacks that I locked myself in the bathroom. I saw my face in the mirror, but I saw it dirty, and I heard that I was told that it was worthless. At that time, I cut my hands and face with a blade. I felt a great need to hurt myself, since I felt guilty about everything that had happened to me.

That night I made the decision to commit suicide, the following Sunday, jumping off a bridge in the city of Lawrence. I would take advantage of it when my grandmother goes to church. During that time, I would go to the place and get off the bridge. That way I would end my life. The days passed, Sunday arrived, and I was determined to complete what was planned: to finish everything, according to me. Unusual things happened that day. When I sat at the table to have breakfast with my grandmother, she talked to me and told me how much she loved me, that she wanted to look very happy. She asked me to accompany her to church that day, along with my aunt, her husband and my cousin, who was small at that time.

I didn't want to go, since I had planned to end my life that day, but I decided to accompany them, because I knew it would be the last time, I would be with them. In my plans I was to go to church and leave before the service ended. That morning, before leaving for church, I had already left a letter addressed to my family explaining the reasons for my decision and saying goodbye to them. In the church I was very anxious, looking at the time to leave, but something strange happened to me. While I was in worship, my heart was beating fast, like never before. I wanted to cry and surrender and be free, but it was a fight against demons that persecuted me wherever I went. They told me: "Don't cry. What you feel is not real. It was God who allowed all your suffering. You must kill yourself to take revenge on everyone and that they are now the ones who suffer."

During the worship service, I tried to get up and leave several times, but something held me back with great force. It was like hitting an invisible wall that wouldn't let me escape. That day, there was a special guest (Elizabeth), a young woman filled with the power and authority of God. She was preaching and I could barely hear her because the demons were disturbing my mind, and I could only hear them. I remember that she began to rebuke, and I managed to catch part of the sermon.

At that moment, a voice told me, "Leave now." I got up and walked towards the church exit. Elizabeth, with authority, said, "Don't go." When I turned around, I saw her pointing her finger at me, but I kept walking towards the exit. With even more authority, she said, "Young girl, do not leave. God is calling you." In that instant, I returned to my seat and thought about waiting for the preacher to pray so I could leave without her noticing. When she called for prayers, I stood up to leave, but she called me by my name and said, "Heidy, come to the front, I have a message for you." She prayed for me and cried alongside me. I felt like someone finally understood me.

She placed her hand on my heart and said to me, "You have suffered greatly, you have cried a lot. I understand your pain and I am here with you. I will heal you. Although you had planned to end your life today, I am your God, who loves you. Today, I lift you up and give your life. Allow me to enter your heart. You have felt alone, but I have always been there. You have turned your back on me, but I love you. You are my child, Heidy. Open your heart and allow me to restore you," and then she hugged me tightly. I felt some relief and decided not to end my life that day. In the evening, when I arrived home, I tore up the letter I had written and shared with my family.

However, there were parts inside me that I didn't want anyone to touch, not even God. I didn't want to forgive my father, and even less confront him to let him know the immense damage he had caused me. I also didn't want to leave the group of friends I would get high with. In this way, I couldn't be fully free because I clung to revenge and hatred towards Alfredo and my father.

At that time as a teenager, among friends we talked about boys and sexuality. They told their experiences and expectations about their first time. I didn't talk much about it, and I tried to stay calm. Inside I cried and asked myself: "What do I say? What was my first time? Was it with my dad or with Alfredo?", and that gave me a great shame, at the same time that I felt disgusted with myself. I pretended to laugh, but inside and in my room, I cried. I didn't understand why those things had happened to me, and that made me hate myself: I hated my body and everything about me.

Time has passed. I was sinking deeper and deeper, not knowing that it was because of the lack of forgiveness. It came at a point when I drank alcohol at all hours of the day. I cut classes at school to go get high, to the point that I was suspended. That year I was supposed to graduate from 8th grade, but they didn't allow me to. Nothing mattered to me.

Classes ended and during the holidays my condition worsened, since from early in the morning I went out with friends, most of them adults who provided me with drugs. I got high and got drunk constantly wanting to forget all my past, but there was a void in me that nothing and no one filled.

A NEW STAGE

FLEE ALSO FROM YOUTHFUL PASSIONS, AND FOLLOWS JUSTICE, FAITH, LOVE AND PEACE, WITH WHICH WITH A CLEAN HEART, THEY CALL ON THE LORD. 2 TIMOTHY 2:2

I started attending parties and meeting older people. This allowed me to have access to more drugs and alcohol, and I went out more frequently. One day, I decided to leave my grandmother's house to experience new things. My family didn't know where I had gone, and eventually, I was reported as missing. I didn't really care; I was completely lost.

Although I sometimes missed my grandmother and found some enjoyment in my freedom, I had no set schedule to return to the house where I was staying. Sometimes I would spend whole days going from one party to another. Inside me, there was a lot of pain, resentment, and a great emptiness that I tried to fill in the ways the world offered me. Deep down, I knew I wasn't doing the right thing and that my lifestyle didn't please God. Months later, after a party, I started feeling sick: I vomited, had a severe headache, and felt extremely tired, but I thought these were normal symptoms. So, I ignored them and continued with my routine.

One day, I decided to call a friend, who informed me that my family had been looking for me and now knew where I was. She warned me that if I didn't return soon, they would do everything possible to have Enrique (the owner of the apartment where I was staying) arrested, as I was underage.

I spoke with Enrique and decided to call my grandmother. She was very happy to hear that I was okay and asked me to come back home. She also told me that they would not press charges against Enrique and that I needed to visit my family in Puerto Rico. I returned to my grandmother and weeks later, I went on vacation to Puerto Rico to visit my mom and siblings. It was beautiful to see them again after being away for so long.

Days and weeks went by, and my mom noticed changes in my body and behavior. One day she said to me, "Heidy, when was your last period?" I couldn't remember, but I knew it had been more than a month. Then she asked me if I had been sexually active with someone, and I told her yes. "It seems like you might be pregnant," she said, "because your body is changing. You look tired all the time and your breasts are growing." In that moment, I fell silent and felt a lot of fear, as I had dreamt of giving birth to a girl, but I didn't dare say anything.

My mom decided to go buy a pregnancy test. When

she came back, she said, "Here it is. You have to take it early in the morning, as soon as you wake up." The next morning, I woke up very early and took the pregnancy test, which turned out positive. I showed it to my mom, and she became very concerned. I felt so scared to tell my boyfriend. He didn't want to take any responsibility, so I decided to stay and live with my mom during the pregnancy.

Several weeks passed and I went to the first medical appointment. Looking at the ultrasound, I was told that I was more than two months pregnant and that I was at high risk, that I had placenta previa and that I should rest. When I heard the sound of the heart for the first time, something inside me changed. I quit smoking and felt for the first time that my life made sense. My pregnancy progressed and my daughter's father decided to move with his parents to Cidra, Puerto Rico, to be closer.

Enrique used drugs and didn't provide what I needed during my pregnancy: he spent everything on drugs. I remember that on one occasion I spent several days without eating anything solid. He cried in despair and had severe pain as a result of hunger. Sometimes I was used, or I set out to compare the drugs to people so that they could give me some money for the favor and with that buy something to eat. God saved me on several occasions from falling prey.

One way or another, God always put the feeling in

my family, they sent money to my mom, and she showed up with something to buy, just when she needed it most.

Time passed and my pregnancy progressed. One day I felt very strange. I was in that all day, feeling pain and discomfort. At night the pain was very intense. When I arrived at the hospital, I was told that I was in labor. I was sent to a special hospital, since my pregnancy had been brought forward and my baby was premature. His arrival was not easy, but he brought so much happiness to my life that nothing else mattered to me. At the age of sixteen, I was the mother of a beautiful girl.

My mom came to meet her granddaughter and I went to spend a week with her at her house. He asked me to stay, since he knew the situation with my daughter's father. A month after my daughter was born, the father began to sell her milk for drugs, so I went with my mom. But he continued to live without God. On one occasion I moved to a room in Guaynabo, PR, in that place many drug addicts lived, and some traffickers rented rooms to pack the drugs. At first everything seemed to be fine, but as the weeks went by and I started using drugs again.

Over time I went back to drinking alcohol, smoking and using drugs. Unlike before, this time the consumption was higher, since it helped several traffickers prepare the drug and pack it to sell it. They, in return, gave me the pure drug, so I became extremely addicted. Sometimes I found myself in difficult situations: one of them asked me for sex in exchange for the drug. On one occasion I was very close to injecting the drug with some friends, when my daughter began to cry and I went to take care of her, which prevented her from injecting me.

What I didn't know at the time is that God was freeing me, since, as the weeks went by, one of those who were sharing the syringe died of AIDS, and I could have been affected. Once again God took care of me, even though I didn't deserve it. At that time, I spent days without eating, since everything was for drugs. When I couldn't stand the hunger anymore, I went to the zafacones and ate the garbage I found. Over time, I became very friendly with a trafficker. He was much older than me. I worked for him packing the drug. He was a well-known man with a lot of money: he had his own boats and several houses. He always brought me gifts, took me to eat, bought things for my daughter and provided me with large amounts of drugs to use. As time went by, my daughter's dad began to hurt me physically, it was no longer just verbal abuse.

I didn't dare to talk to anyone, not even my mom. The only person I told him about the physical abuse was my dad, because I saw him frequently when he visited since he was a friend of the owner where I lived. My dad told me that it was normal for there to be fights in the couple and that I had to endure as a woman. He kissed me on the forehead and went to buy drugs and alcohol with Enrique.

I was tired of living that life, but I didn't know how to get out of it. As the days went by, my mom arrived by surprise where I lived. Someone had called her and told her the condition in which I lived. She asked me to give her my daughter so that the baby would not suffer, but I refused to give her, and I agreed to go with my mom with my daughter and look for a better life for both of them.

I wanted to be free of drugs and give my daughter the life she deserved. I had to distance myself from many people and moved from Puerto Rico to the United States, with my grandmother. At that time, she weighed less than eighty pounds and was very affected, physically and emotionally. When I moved in with my grandmother, I began to get better. Things happened in my life: I had my second daughter. I visited churches, but I didn't want a commitment to God. In this way, as the years go by, I re-enlived my life. I was married for ten years, and I had my other two daughters. God gave me four princesses that changed my life.

AT THE EDGE OF DEATH

AND JEHOVAH GOES AHEAD OF YOU; HE WILL BE WITH YOU, HE WILL NOT LEAVE YOU, NOR HE WILL FORSAKE; DON'T BE AFRAID OR BE INTIMIDATED. DEUTERONOMY 31:8

In my marriage, I wasn't happy. My husband and I had many differences, and our personalities were very different. We didn't share things in common or religious beliefs. We had many problems, including infidelity, among other things, which led us to divorce. Over time, I started attending a church. I would go to parties on weekends and get drunk, but every Sunday, I would attend church. I pretended to be happy when, in reality, I felt lonely, empty, and tired of trying, over and over again, to change and improve my life.

Eventually, I met a man named Diego. We became friends and then decided to become a couple. There were things about him that seemed strange to me, but he appeared to be a good person. He wasn't a Christian, but he knew about God. On several occasions, we drifted apart and stopped talking to each other. I had several dreams in which this man would get off a train and, upon picking him up, he would shoot me multiple times and leave the scene, leaving me dead. I knew that God was warning me of danger, but every time Diego sought me out, I would get involved with him again. My family had known him since childhood and told me that he had many behavioral issues, but in my rebellion and frustration, and wanting to fill the emptiness in my heart, I didn't listen to them. Time continued to pass, and everything that seemed to be going well and at peace turned into a nightmare that God had warned me about.

One day, I noticed a strange behavior in him, and then that afternoon, he found any reason to argue, hurting me with very hurtful words, and then he physically hit me very hard. That filled me with a lot of fear. We separated for a long time, and then he asked for my forgiveness. He confessed to me that his reaction had been because he used to be a user of drugs (crack) and that when he needed them, he would become violent. Since I hadn't healed things from my past that I was struggling with internally, I would fall back into the same cycle.

Despite attending church, I didn't lead a life of prayer or seeking God, and I surrounded myself with friends who further distanced me from Him. One night, I cried alone in my room and talked to God. I asked Him why so many things were happening. Each hurtful word that Diego said to me caused such immense pain that I wished for death. I remembered the words of people close to me during my childhood, such as those who said that no man would ever love or respect me because I was marked and tainted from a young age. All of this deeply affected me and made me believe that I had to accept it, that my life was destined for abuse.

I felt the shame of leading a double life, knowing that I wasn't seeking or honoring God as I should, and the daily pain I endured prevented me from fully surrendering to Him. For a while, I decided not to attend any church. The physical abuse inflicted by Diego was incredibly severe. He would drag me by my hair until it was pulled out from the roots, leaving my scalp bleeding. I felt every bite on my body. I could count each toothmark on my skin, each blow to my face (which I had to cover with makeup to hide from others what I was going through). He would spit in my face in front of people, break my lips, and kick me, among many other things.

I remember that one of those nights the blows were so and so strong... Despite being lying on the ground and without the strength to fight, she took one of her Nike boots and gave me so hard that it left the mark on my skin. At that moment the girls came in screaming and crying, and I could see growing in their eyes the same fear that I had: the fear of losing their mother. They often called me from school to make sure that I was alive, since they were afraid that, when I returned, I would be dead. On several occasions he was imprisoned, but I ended up forgiving him, since, since my childhood, I grew up thinking that abuse was something normal and that part of the forgiveness was to receive that person in your life again and again.

That's why it's very important to heal wounds before entering a relationship. Over time I began to go to a church together, in which I felt something that for many years I had not felt it was the power of God and his Holy Spirit. In this church I found shelter and I felt that I was not alone. Despite the fact that the physical, verbal and emotional abuse continued at home, I had the faith and hope that God would give me the strength to get out of that situation. I felt dirty. I thought I was going to go crazy, and, on many occasions, I planned to end my life and leave my daughters with my family. The enemy used people, doubt, lack of forgiveness and fear to complete the damage he had caused me since my childhood, and in this way stop me on the way so that God's work would not be completed in my life. Even worse, that my daughters were also marked, since there are curses that must be broken in the name of Jesus, so that things are not repeated in the lives of our children. Several events were repeated in terms of domestic violence.

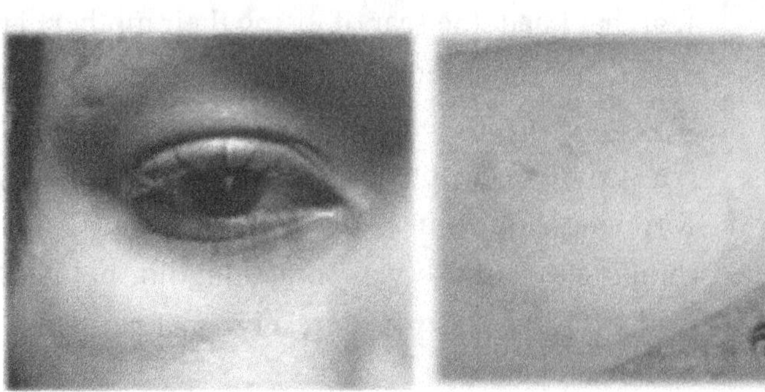

I was already determined to surrender completely to God because I recognized that I no longer wanted to continue the lifestyle I was living, and above all, I longed to heal and be free.

One day, he hit me again because I came home late from a vigil. He broke my lip and left me with a swollen eye. I was filled with fear and very weak due to a medical treatment I was undergoing. I told him not to hit me anymore or I would call the police. Something had changed inside me; I no longer saw him in the same way, and I had grown stronger in God.

That night, I called the police because he also hit one of my daughters. He escaped before the police arrived. From that day on, I promised myself that I would no longer tolerate any more abuse, and I prepared myself emotionally and financially to stay alone with my daughters. I continued attending church, but there were still areas of my life that needed healing and many chains to break, such as the smoking addiction.

I remember one Friday, around 8:00 AM, after dropping off my daughters at school, I decided to go to the church I used to attend to pray. That day, I poured out my heart to God and asked for His help. Some brothers and sisters prayed for me and invited me to a women's retreat the following day, Saturday. When I got home, I spent time thinking and reflecting on my life. I decided to fully surrender to God and let Him take control.

On Saturday, I attended the women's retreat and

God spoke to me through two sisters. In that moment, I was set free from the smoking addiction. In that church, I met people who became my family and helped me in the process. From that day on, my life completely changed. I was freed from resentment, addictions, and the cycle of abuse that haunted me and threatened my daughters' lives. I had the courage to press charges and obtain a restraining order. He continued evading the police until they finally arrested him. After a few weeks, he was arrested. That's when the complete restoration process of my life, and my daughters' lives, began. It was a very painful process in which we sought psychological and spiritual help. He received a long sentence, and we never got back together.

NO MORE PUPPET

HE GIVES EFFORT TO THE TIRED AND MULTIPLIES THE FORCES TO THOSE WHO HAVE NONE. ISAIAH 40:29

Perhaps you wonder what a puppet is. A puppet is a person with weak character and little willpower, who allows themselves to be manipulated by someone else. At some point, we have all been puppets of Satan (consciously or unconsciously, in one way or another). It is not until we know Jesus Christ that we can realize this sad reality.

When I decided to leave this abusive relationship, the Lord opened my eyes and gradually broke the chains that Satan had imposed on me. Many thought, even myself, that it would be impossible to break free from this vicious cycle of abuse, where my innocence became a victim of the evilness of man. Something inside me filled me with strength and reminded me that I should not allow Satan to continue playing with me. I grew tired of feeling insignificant when I knew that I was bought with the price of blood. I became tired of being just another victim. I grew tired of feeling like a punching bag for Satan. I grew tired of seeing how the enemy tried to repeat history in the lives of my daughters. I grew tired and I decided to rise up and not let this opportunity pass.

I attended a congregation, but I knew that if I wanted change, that would not be enough. I began an intense search at home. Rising up was not easy. Although I wished for everything to happen overnight, it wasn't so. God dealt with me little by little until He healed and broke everything, and although it hurt and many times I thought of dying, the Holy Spirit gave me strength.

On one occasion, God told me He was going to deal with me alone, that it was going to be a very personal matter. I didn't understand, but over time, and seeking

His presence, I realized what it meant. In intimacy, God broke my chains and showed me that He was waging war against me.

Some of the things God taught me were forgiveness, confusion, fear, insecurity, depression, suicide, addictions, fear of commitment, generational curses, homosexuality, changes, spiritual warfare, and lack of trust. I understood that I would not find joy, love, compassion, and hope in the world, but rather pain, to the point of being on the verge of death. The only thing that kept me alive was the grace and mercy of God.

As a result of many years of suffering, it was very difficult for me to rise up and believe in myself. There were moments of despair. I wanted to heal and be free. I wished that God would heal my wounds instantly, without having to go through the process. There are wounds so deep that they take time to heal. Memories invaded my mind. A deep sadness flooded my life. Guilt and doubt had become my companions. I felt it was impossible to rise up and be a joyful woman, full of life, with dreams and hopes... The person I once was. It was as if life was determined to steal away the smile and joy that come from God.

Unbeknownst to me, I was living a life of appearances: pretending to be fine and always offering a smile to everyone around me, but in my solitude, I felt and wished for death. It was easy for me to forgive those who had hurt me, but I couldn't forgive myself. I felt responsible for everything that had happened in my life. Guilt was a burden I carried everywhere. My self-esteem was in the gutter. That's why it was so difficult for me to rise up and believe in myself.

One day, I made the decision to go back to studying, hoping that by improving myself, I would feel better. Nothing worked. Despite going to church, I hadn't been completely set free until I recognized and understood that I needed to be freed from the invisible chains that bound my life. Those voices that spoke to me, telling me that I couldn't rise up, and those memories that caused me pain were demons that had a hold on me and tormented me. Only the power of God could truly set me free. Many times, it is easy for us to defeat the giants that wage war against us, but it becomes almost impossible to be free from those small things that weave themselves into our minds and hearts. Things like fear, doubt, rejection, deep-rooted bitterness, that sometimes we don't even know are there because the enemy gradually blinds us so that we can't see clearly.

On various occasions, God spoke to me and told me that He wanted to use me in a special way, but I needed to allow Him to enter those areas that needed to be restored. Sometimes, it is we ourselves who don't allow God to work in us because we refuse to accept the condition, we are in. In my case, I thought I had forgiven my father and those people who had left their mark on me, when in reality, I hadn't forgiven them from the heart, and this hindered my complete liberation.

One day, while praying, I heard a voice asking me, "Have you forgiven your father?" I responded that I had forgiven him. Then that voice said to me, "Why don't you pray for him, that he may be saved and repent of his sins?" I cried and asked God for forgiveness. In that moment, I prayed for my father and for every person who had hurt me. I asked for mercy for them and for them to be set free and transformed. This helped me find relief in my life and allowed God to work.

The process of healing and liberation, in my case, was the most difficult thing I have ever experienced. During this process, I psychologically relived moments of despair and intense pain. At times, I could feel the physical pain I had endured. It was through confrontation and personal brokenness that I was able to receive healing and liberation.

God worked in my life little by little. He first addressed the areas affected since my childhood, such as lack of self-love, mistrust, insecurity, among others. The most challenging area to tackle was the wounds left by domestic violence. These wounds marked my heart and contaminated me. It was a deep wound that wouldn't allow anyone to come near it. Gradually, I began opening my heart for God to heal that area.

In everyday life, there are different processes to heal

physical wounds. There are various types of wounds. Some are a result of accidents, while others are caused by surgical interventions. Any break in the skin is a wound. Without proper care, there is a risk of infection (an infection occurs when germs enter a part of the body and multiply, sometimes causing diseases that can affect other areas). To avoid infections, it is necessary to care for the wound correctly.

The deeper, larger, or dirtier the wound is, the more care it requires, and the longer it takes to heal. Doctors don't always close wounds immediately. If there is a possibility of contamination, they leave it open to clean it. The same happens to us sometimes. The wound remains open due to an infection, like unforgiveness, etc.

It is necessary for the wound to remain open until we make room for God to enter and completely heal it, without leaving any contamination within us. Some wounds require stitches to join two separate layers. These stitches are removed days later for the wound to heal, and their removal can cause pain and discomfort. Similarly, the wounds of the soul caused by different circumstances we go through.

We can compare infections with those things that grow inside us, slowly creating a network that affects other areas. They become a vicious circle: hatred and the desire for revenge, among other things. These mark our lives in one way or another and require a healing process.

They are painful processes but necessary ones in which we must allow God to come in and start removing those stitches and disinfecting each wound. Perhaps those stitches are the lack of forgiveness, lack of self-love, mistrust, doubt, fear, among many things that overwhelm us and keep us stagnant.

When we desire to be healthy and free from the things of the past, it is necessary to forgive from the heart. We must forgive those who have hurt us, but also forgive ourselves. Personally, I felt responsible for my parents' divorce. If we refuse to forgive and hold on to being victims instead of survivors, we allow hatred to take root, which will hinder the work of the Holy Spirit within us. We may feel the presence of God, speak in tongues, and perform miracles, but still be bound. Living with resentment and guilt draws us away from God and halts our spiritual growth.

One day, I realized that it was necessary to surrender everything to God. Through humility and repentance, I bowed before Christ and reconciled with Him. Although I attended church, my life was still tied to worldly things. Gradually, my life was transformed. I sought God in spirit and truth, and desired to live a life of both internal and external holiness. I committed myself to fasting, and during that fast, chains were broken, and I understood that there were generational curses pursuing me from which I needed to renounce.

I had to go through moments of scarcity. I went through deserts and experienced the acceptance of my brokenness and the silence of God in my life. I sought God at all times and in all places. His presence became everything to me. I have seen the hand of God working in a special and unexplainable way in my life. For Him, nothing is impossible. He is always willing and waiting for us with open arms. His love and mercy are endless. It is a love that surpasses all understanding. Something I have learned is that we are the ones who hinder God from flowing in our lives. We are our greatest obstacle for God's purpose to be fulfilled. Many times, we allow doubts and pain to prevent us from pleasing God and praising Him with all our hearts.

When we surrender everything into His hands, all things work for good. There may be things we do not understand in that moment, but we must have faith in God and be certain that everything He allows in our lives is for testimony and for His own glorification. The worst thing we can do is blame God for the bad things that happen to us. The evil in the world is a result of man's wickedness and sin. God has given us free will, and each one is responsible for their actions and will be held accountable to Him. We should never assume the role of victims but of survivors. We must give thanks to God for pulling us out of the mud and never look back.

By surrendering everything to God, I had new experiences in my spiritual life. I felt Him molding my life and removing everything that was not pleasing to Him.

CONFUSION

Confusion is the lack of order or clarity, and it enters into our lives when we place our trust in the wrong person. We must understand that the Bible clearly teaches us that God is not the author of confusion and that a source of confusion is sin (Daniel 9:8-9). However, we must cling more and more to God every day and put into practice this proverb: "Trust in the Lord with all your heart, and do not lean on your own understanding. In all your ways acknowledge him, and he will make straight your paths. Be not wise in your own eyes; fear the Lord and turn away from evil; for it will be healing to your flesh and refreshment to your bones" (Proverbs 3:5-8).

FEAR

We all know what fear is. In one way or another, we have faced situations where we have felt fear for different reasons. However, very few can truly get rid of it. There is only one thing that can truly eliminate all fear from us, and that is the love of God. Not just knowing that He loves us but allowing Him to perfect His love in us (1 John 4:18). Fear not only imprisons us, but its end is the lake of fire (Revelation 21:8). No matter how strong our fears may be, we cannot run away from them but must confront them under the guidance of the Holy Spirit.

INSECURITY

Due to the past, the world has lost its identity, and this is the root of insecurity. Christ not only came to earth to die for our sins and conquer death, but He came to reclaim what had been lost. The only way we can feel security in our lives is through Christ Jesus, for He is "the way, the truth, and the life," and no one comes to the Father except through Him (John 14:6).

DEPRESSION

Depression is a widely spread disorder, affecting millions of people, both Christians and non-Christians alike. Those who suffer from depression may experience intense feelings of sadness, anger, hopelessness, fatigue, and a variety of other symptoms. They may begin to feel worthless and even think about suicide, losing interest in things and people they once enjoyed. God gives encouragement to the depressed. He may not remove all your problems, but He will give you the strength to carry on. We must strive to be of the Holy Spirit and bear fruit through joy. We can rejoice and trust in God, knowing that all things will work together for good. Psalm 34:18 says, "The Lord is near to the brokenhearted and saves the crushed in spirit."

SUICIDE

Many people consider suicide as a solution to their problems. They believe that by ending their lives, they will also end their struggles, but in reality, it leads them to eternal suffering in hell. Suicide is the result of intense emotional pain.

If we examine the fruits of the Spirit (love, joy, peace, patience, kindness, goodness, faithfulness, gentleness, and self-control), suicide, which is a deep hatred towards one's own life, is not a good fruit but an act of the flesh (Galatians 5:17-21). We are temples of God, and we must take care of ourselves (1 Corinthians 3:16-17). Satan uses pain to make us feel worthless and convince us that we are a mistake, pushing us towards suicide and the loss of our souls in hell.

ADDICTIONS

We must recognize the value we have in God's hands and refute anything that tells us otherwise. Addictions, whether to drugs, alcohol, medication, smoking, pornography, gambling, food, etc., are ways in which humans try to find refuge or temporary solutions to things that hurt us, and we want to forget. The sin of these addictions leads us to death, and what starts as something small eventually consumes us. The only way to overcome these addictions is to acknowledge that we are in the wrong and surrender to God for His help.

Overcoming an addiction is a lengthy process because when Satan sees that you are determined to change, he comes to tempt you again and again until he sees that you are truly firm: "Submit yourselves therefore

to God. Resist the devil, and he will flee from you"
(James 4:7).

GENERATIONAL CURSES

A curse is an expression or set of words that invoke
or wish harm upon a person. When we talk about
generational curses, we refer to a curse pronounced by
someone influenced by Satan which remains active from
generation to generation. That's why we see many
women who were abused as children also having abused
daughters, or when a young person is addicted to drugs,
the father and grandfather were too.

We must be very careful with what comes out of our
mouths because many times we curse our children and
future generations without even realizing it. How many
times have we heard parents telling their children that
they are worthless?

Things like these become curses. Upon conversion,
it is necessary to break and renounce any curse that may
be following us and fast so that the Lord may break any
corrupted word against us.

HOMOSEXUALITY

Homosexuality is the sexual desire or physical
attraction towards people of the same sex, and it goes
against God's will and his established order since
creation (Genesis 1:27-28; Leviticus 18:22). It is

considered a sin in the eyes of God, but it is important to remember that God loves each one of us, even though He abhors our sins. God is willing to forgive us and cleanse us. We just need to confess our sins and ask Him to transform us and remove all confusion from our minds.

FORGIVENESS

Forgiveness is the act of forgiving (excusing, forgetting) another person for hurting us or saying something offensive. At some point in our lives, we all have had to forgive someone who has hurt us. You may have to forgive people who haven't even repented or asked for forgiveness, which can be very challenging. Forgiving someone voluntarily is a benefit to ourselves because by forgiving, we break the chains of sadness, bitterness, depression, and hatred, and we allow God to enter our lives and heal us completely. Forgiveness sets us free and opens the doors to spiritual prisons. Lack of forgiveness can also affect our health, causing heart problems, hypertension, anxiety, and panic attacks, among others.

By not forgiving, we condemn our generation to live in bitterness because everyone gives what they have inside. A wounded person wounds, and a bitter person fills those around them with bitterness. Without forgiveness, we cannot love in the right way because we carry burdens from the past that end up hurting people who are not guilty of our wounds. Jesus gave us the greatest example by forgiving, loving, and praying for those who have hurt us.

OVERCOMING TRAUMAS

In life, we all go through traumas or situations that mark our lives in one way or another. These can include the abandonment of a parent, rejection from a family member, teasing from peers, physical, sexual, or emotional abuse, among others.

It is necessary to heal. The healing process is different for each person, but we all need God for this healing to be complete and effective. It is important to recognize our condition, accept that we are wounded, and confess it, whether with a professional, a spiritual leader, and above all, talk to God about it.

Accepting and seeking solutions and changes are the only way to work on those areas. In the Bible, we find many stories of people with different needs and illnesses. Each and every one of them achieved their miracle by recognizing that they needed freedom and healing. They all got tired of living in the condition they were in and sought their miracle. After recognizing and admitting that we need help, we must take action. Let's surrender everything to God, let's surrender ourselves, and allow Him to heal every area of our lives.

SPIRITUAL WARFARE

All the points we touched above are fought by doing spiritual warfare. As believers we are in a constant war. The enemy uses people to hurt us, but it's not them, but the demons and the malice's in them. Satan came to steal, kill and destroy. That's what he wants to do with each of us, so we have to put on the armor of God (Ephesians 6, 10-18) and fight for our salvation, against every lie of the devil and give up our past.

I learned all these things in intimacy with God, and I had to be very processed. I was able to forgive my father and all the men who had abused me, and now I can pray for them, wish them well and that one day they will know God and be saved. God changed my life completely and I can see his greatness in my life. Since I was a child, I had a dream in which, after a long chase, a man, with a shining light, waited for me with open arms and healed me of my wounds. Likewise, God was waiting for me to transform myself inside and out. Every tear has its reward, and every process has a purpose. I couldn't have been the woman I am today without every process I had to go through. Today I can say that I am blessed with a family dedicated to the Lord. But what would have happened if I had been satisfied with my lifestyle, with the fact that the world saw me as a simple victim of sexual and physical abuse? I would still be in the same pond, maybe dead and my soul lost in hell.

We can't let the pain and wounds blind us and stop us. Don't let the wounds you have in you make you forget the Almighty God. Today I want you to know that everything the devil used to destroy you, God will use to mold you. That every tear you shed God wants to use to bless you and that you witness his transforming power and his infinite love. We cannot see ourselves as just one more victim, but as survivors who have received an undeserved gift. He loved us first, and that's why we must serve him and let him take us in his hands and us the way he wants.

Despite everything I experienced, I can say something today: beyond all my wounds, I am a witness to the power of God and how he can transform us. Someone in whom no one saw value, he turned it into a precious pearl. It's time to start seeing each other beyond our wounds!

Since I surrendered completely, I have seen God restore my life. God has given me a beautiful family and most importantly he has given me forgiveness, salvation and eternal life.

Today I invite you to open your heart and invite God into your life. May you allow his Holy Spirit to dwell in you. Let it enter your house and transform everything. Give yourself up completely.

If you want to pray, I'll join you right now...

Loving Father, my Lord and Savior. I humble myself before you, recognizing that I am a sinner. And I need to be free in you. I repent of each and every one of my sins. Help me to forgive and heal every area in me.

I give you everything I have and everything I am.

Clean me and I'll be clean. Break the chains that tie my life. I release the forgiveness to all those who have hurt me. And I apologize to those I have hurt on the way.

From today I want to serve you. Write my name in the book of life. And that it will never be deleted again.

Help me to see as you see and to live in holiness by obeying your word. In the powerful name of Jesus,

Amen!

www.ingramcontent.com/pod-product-compliance
Lightning Source LLC
Chambersburg PA
CBHW072113150726
47999CB00005B/2015